EMMANUEL JOSEPH

The Psychology of Influence, Public Speaking, Leadership, and the Art of Taking Action

Copyright © 2025 by Emmanuel Joseph

All rights reserved. No part of this publication may be reproduced, stored or transmitted in any form or by any means, electronic, mechanical, photocopying, recording, scanning, or otherwise without written permission from the publisher. It is illegal to copy this book, post it to a website, or distribute it by any other means without permission.

First edition

This book was professionally typeset on Reedsy.
Find out more at reedsy.com

Contents

1 Chapter 1: The Foundations of Influence   1
2 Chapter 2: The Power of Storytelling   3
3 Chapter 3: The Art of Persuasion   5
4 Chapter 4: The Dynamics of Leadership   7
5 Chapter 5: The Role of Communication in Influence   9
6 Chapter 6: The Psychology of Public Speaking   11
7 Chapter 7: Building Confidence as a Leader   13
8 Chapter 8: The Science of Motivation   15
9 Chapter 9: Overcoming Resistance and Building Resilience   17
10 Chapter 10: The Role of Empathy in Influence   19
11 Chapter 11: The Ethics of Influence   21
12 Chapter 12: The Impact of Social Proof   23
13 Chapter 13: The Art of Negotiation   25
14 Chapter 14: The Role of Emotional Intelligence in Influence   27
15 Chapter 15: The Influence of Culture on Leadership   29
16 Chapter 16: The Role of Technology in Influence   31
17 Chapter 17: Taking Action and Making a Difference   33

1

Chapter 1: The Foundations of Influence

Influence is not a power that a chosen few possess but a skill that anyone can develop. At its core, influence is about understanding human behavior and leveraging that knowledge to motivate others. The roots of influence stretch back to the earliest societies, where leaders emerged based on their ability to persuade and inspire. It involves a blend of psychology, communication, and empathy. By understanding what drives people, one can tailor messages to resonate deeply, creating a sense of connection and trust. In this chapter, we will explore the basic principles of influence, highlighting how they manifest in everyday interactions.

The psychology of influence is grounded in the study of human motivations and behaviors. Psychologists have long studied why people act the way they do and how they can be guided towards desired outcomes. Key concepts such as persuasion, authority, and social proof are essential to mastering influence. Persuasion involves presenting information in a way that aligns with the values and beliefs of the audience. Authority, on the other hand, comes from being perceived as knowledgeable and trustworthy. Social proof leverages the tendency of people to follow the actions of others, especially those they respect or admire.

Effective communication is a cornerstone of influence. It is not just about what you say but how you say it. The tone, body language, and context all play a critical role in how messages are received and interpreted. For instance, a confident and calm demeanor can make your message more convincing. Understanding your audience, their needs, and their expectations allows you to craft your communication to have the maximum impact. Empathy, the ability to understand and share the feelings of others, also enhances your ability to influence by building rapport and trust.

By mastering the fundamentals of influence, individuals can improve their personal and professional lives. Whether it's convincing a colleague to support your project, motivating a team to achieve a common goal, or inspiring an audience through public speaking, the principles of influence are universally applicable. This chapter lays the groundwork for understanding and developing this essential skill, setting the stage for deeper exploration in the following chapters.

2

Chapter 2: The Power of Storytelling

Storytelling is one of the most powerful tools for influence. Stories have been used for centuries to teach, inspire, and connect people. They are a fundamental part of human experience, allowing individuals to share knowledge, culture, and values. A well-told story can captivate an audience, evoke emotions, and leave a lasting impression. In this chapter, we will delve into the art of storytelling, exploring its components and how it can be used to influence effectively.

A compelling story typically has a clear structure: a beginning, middle, and end. The beginning sets the scene and introduces the characters. It draws the audience in and provides context for what is to come. The middle of the story presents the conflict or challenge that the characters face. This is where the tension builds and the audience becomes emotionally invested. The end resolves the conflict and provides closure, leaving the audience with a sense of satisfaction or a call to action.

Emotion plays a critical role in storytelling. People are more likely to remember and be influenced by stories that evoke strong emotions. Whether it's joy, sadness, fear, or anger, emotions make the experience more vivid and memorable. Effective storytellers use various techniques to evoke emotions, such as vivid descriptions, relatable characters, and dramatic tension. By connecting with the audience on an emotional level, the storyteller can create a deeper and more lasting impact.

In addition to structure and emotion, authenticity is essential for successful storytelling. Audiences can easily detect when a story feels forced or insincere. Genuine stories resonate because they reflect real experiences and truths. Authenticity builds trust and credibility, making the audience more receptive to the message. When crafting a story, it's important to stay true to your experiences and values, as well as those of your audience.

3

Chapter 3: The Art of Persuasion

Persuasion is the backbone of influence. It involves presenting arguments and evidence in a way that convinces others to adopt a particular viewpoint or take specific actions. The art of persuasion is not about manipulation but about understanding and addressing the needs and concerns of others. In this chapter, we will explore various techniques and strategies for persuading effectively, drawing from both psychological principles and practical examples.

One of the key elements of persuasion is credibility. People are more likely to be persuaded by someone they perceive as knowledgeable and trustworthy. Building credibility involves demonstrating expertise, being honest, and establishing a track record of reliability. This can be achieved through clear communication, providing evidence and examples, and being transparent about intentions and motivations. Credibility creates a foundation of trust that makes the audience more receptive to the persuasive message.

Another important aspect of persuasion is understanding the audience. Different people are motivated by different things, and effective persuasion requires tailoring the message to the specific audience. This involves listening to their needs and concerns, addressing their objections, and highlighting the benefits that matter most to them. By showing empathy and genuinely engaging with the audience, the persuader can create a sense of connection and make the message more compelling.

The use of logical arguments and emotional appeals is also crucial in persuasion. Logical arguments are based on facts, evidence, and reasoning. They provide a solid foundation for the persuasive message and help to establish credibility. Emotional appeals, on the other hand, tap into the audience's feelings and values. They create a sense of urgency, motivation, and connection. Balancing logical arguments with emotional appeals can create a powerful and persuasive message.

Effective persuasion also involves the strategic use of language and rhetoric. The choice of words, tone, and style can greatly influence how a message is received. Techniques such as repetition, storytelling, and rhetorical questions can make the message more engaging and memorable. Being aware of cultural and contextual factors is also important, as different audiences may respond differently to various persuasion techniques.

4

Chapter 4: The Dynamics of Leadership

L eadership is closely intertwined with the ability to influence others. Great leaders are often great influencers, capable of inspiring and guiding their teams towards common goals. Leadership is not just about giving orders but about creating a vision, building relationships, and motivating others. In this chapter, we will explore the dynamics of leadership and how it relates to influence, drawing from both historical examples and modern theories.

At its core, leadership is about creating a vision and inspiring others to follow it. A compelling vision provides direction and purpose, giving people something to strive for. Great leaders are able to articulate their vision clearly and passionately, making it relatable and achievable for their teams. They also demonstrate commitment to the vision through their actions, setting an example for others to follow.

Building relationships is another critical aspect of leadership. Effective leaders understand the importance of trust, respect, and collaboration. They invest time in getting to know their team members, understanding their strengths and weaknesses, and providing support and guidance. By fostering a positive and inclusive environment, leaders can create a sense of belonging and loyalty, which in turn enhances their influence.

Motivation is a key component of leadership. Great leaders know how to motivate their teams to achieve their best. This involves recognizing and rewarding achievements, providing opportunities for growth and development, and creating a sense of purpose and meaning in the work. Motivation can be both intrinsic, driven by personal satisfaction and fulfillment, and extrinsic, driven by external rewards and recognition. Effective leaders understand the balance between these two types of motivation and use them to inspire their teams.

Leadership also involves making difficult decisions and taking responsibility for the outcomes. Great leaders are not afraid to take risks and make tough choices, even when they are unpopular. They are willing to stand by their decisions and take accountability for their actions. This requires a combination of confidence, resilience, and ethical judgment. By demonstrating these qualities, leaders can earn the respect and trust of their teams, further enhancing their influence.

5

Chapter 5: The Role of Communication in Influence

Communication is the bridge between intention and action. It is through communication that we express our ideas, build relationships, and influence others. Effective communication involves not just the words we use but also our tone, body language, and listening skills. In this chapter, we will explore the role of communication in influence, highlighting key techniques and strategies for effective communication.

Clear and concise communication is essential for influence. When conveying a message, it is important to be clear about the main points and to avoid unnecessary jargon or complexity. This makes the message easier to understand and more impactful. Additionally, being concise ensures that the audience remains engaged and focused on the key points. Using simple and direct language can enhance the clarity and effectiveness of the message.

Non-verbal communication, such as body language and facial expressions, plays a significant role in how messages are received. For example, maintaining eye contact can create a sense of connection and trust, while open body language can make you appear more approachable and confident. Being aware of your non-verbal cues and using them effectively can enhance your ability to influence others.

Active listening is another crucial aspect of effective communication. Listening is not just about hearing the words but understanding the underlying emotions and intentions. By actively listening, you can respond more effectively and build stronger connections. This involves giving your full attention, asking clarifying questions, and providing feedback. Active listening demonstrates empathy and respect, which in turn enhances your influence.

The use of storytelling in communication can also be a powerful tool for influence. As discussed in Chapter 2, stories can captivate an audience and create an emotional connection. By incorporating stories into your communication, you can make your message more relatable and memorable. This can be particularly effective in public speaking, where engaging the audience is key to delivering a powerful message.

6

Chapter 6: The Psychology of Public Speaking

Public speaking is one of the most effective ways to influence a large audience. However, it is also one of the most common fears. Understanding the psychology of public speaking can help individuals overcome their anxiety and deliver impactful presentations. In this chapter, we will explore the psychological aspects of public speaking and provide practical tips for becoming to engaging an audience.

Public speaking anxiety, or glossophobia, is a common issue that affects many people. The fear of speaking in front of others can stem from various sources, such as fear of judgment, fear of failure, or lack of confidence. Understanding the root causes of this anxiety can help individuals address and overcome it. Techniques such as deep breathing, visualization, and positive self-talk can help manage anxiety and improve confidence. Practicing and preparing thoroughly can also reduce anxiety by increasing familiarity with the material and the speaking environment.

The psychology of public speaking also involves understanding the audience. Knowing who you are speaking to and what they care about allows you to tailor your message to their interests and needs. This involves researching the audience, considering their demographics, and identifying their potential concerns or questions. By addressing these factors in your presentation, you can create a more engaging and relevant message.

Engaging the audience is crucial for effective public speaking. This can be achieved through various techniques, such as storytelling, humor, and interactive elements. Using visual aids, such as slides or props, can also enhance engagement and help convey your message more effectively. Maintaining eye contact, using expressive body language, and varying your tone and pace can also keep the audience's attention and make your presentation more dynamic.

Finally, feedback is an essential part of improving public speaking skills. Seeking feedback from others, whether through formal evaluations or informal conversations, can provide valuable insights into your strengths and areas for improvement. Reflecting on your own experiences and identifying what worked well and what could be improved can also help you refine your skills over time.

7

Chapter 7: Building Confidence as a Leader

Confidence is a key trait of effective leaders. It allows them to make decisions, take risks, and inspire others with conviction. However, confidence is not an inherent trait but a skill that can be developed and strengthened over time. In this chapter, we will explore strategies for building and maintaining confidence as a leader, drawing from both psychological principles and practical tips.

Self-awareness is the foundation of confidence. Understanding your strengths and weaknesses, as well as your values and goals, provides a solid basis for building confidence. This involves reflecting on your experiences, seeking feedback from others, and being honest with yourself about your capabilities. By acknowledging your strengths and working on your weaknesses, you can develop a balanced and realistic sense of self-confidence.

Setting and achieving small goals can also help build confidence. By breaking down larger tasks into manageable steps and celebrating each accomplishment, you can create a sense of progress and momentum. This not only boosts confidence but also provides motivation to continue working towards your larger goals. It's important to recognize and celebrate your successes, no matter how small, as they contribute to your overall sense of achievement and confidence.

Developing a growth mindset is another important aspect of building confidence. A growth mindset involves believing that your abilities and intelligence can be developed through effort and learning. This mindset encourages you to embrace challenges, learn from failures, and persist in the face of setbacks. By adopting a growth mindset, you can build resilience and confidence in your ability to grow and improve as a leader.

Finally, seeking support and mentorship can also enhance your confidence. Surrounding yourself with supportive and encouraging individuals can provide valuable guidance, feedback, and encouragement. Mentors, in particular, can offer insights and advice based on their own experiences, helping you navigate challenges and build confidence in your abilities. Building a strong support network can provide the encouragement and motivation needed to develop and maintain confidence as a leader.

8

Chapter 8: The Science of Motivation

Motivation is the driving force behind action. Understanding what motivates people can help leaders and influencers guide others towards achieving their goals. Motivation is a complex and multifaceted concept that involves both internal and external factors. In this chapter, we will explore the science of motivation, examining various theories and strategies for motivating yourself and others.

Intrinsic motivation comes from within and is driven by personal satisfaction, interest, and fulfillment. People who are intrinsically motivated engage in activities because they find them enjoyable or meaningful. This type of motivation is often more sustainable and effective than extrinsic motivation, which is driven by external rewards or pressures. Understanding and fostering intrinsic motivation can help individuals stay committed and engaged in their pursuits.

Extrinsic motivation, on the other hand, involves external rewards such as money, recognition, or praise. While extrinsic motivation can be effective in certain situations, it is often less sustainable in the long term. Over-reliance on external rewards can lead to a lack of intrinsic motivation and a decrease in overall satisfaction and engagement. Effective leaders understand the balance between intrinsic and extrinsic motivation and use both to inspire and motivate others.

Goal-setting is a powerful tool for motivation. Setting clear, specific, and achievable goals provides direction and a sense of purpose. Goals should be challenging yet attainable, and should be broken down into smaller, manageable steps. This allows individuals to track their progress and stay motivated by celebrating each milestone. Additionally, setting deadlines and creating accountability can enhance motivation and ensure that goals are pursued with commitment and focus.

Creating a positive and supportive environment can also enhance motivation. Providing encouragement, recognizing achievements, and fostering a sense of community can create a motivating atmosphere. This involves understanding the needs and preferences of individuals and creating an environment that supports their growth and development. By cultivating a positive and motivating environment, leaders can inspire others to achieve their best.

9

Chapter 9: Overcoming Resistance and Building Resilience

Resistance to change and challenges is a natural part of human behavior. However, overcoming resistance and building resilience is essential for effective influence and leadership. In this chapter, we will explore strategies for addressing resistance and developing resilience, drawing from psychological principles and practical tips.

Understanding the root causes of resistance is the first step in overcoming it. Resistance often stems from fear of the unknown, loss of control, or a perceived threat to one's identity or values. By identifying and addressing these underlying concerns, leaders can help individuals feel more comfortable and open to change. This involves listening to their concerns, providing clear information, and involving them in the decision-making process.

Building resilience involves developing the ability to adapt and recover from setbacks. Resilience is not an inherent trait but a skill that can be cultivated through practice and experience. Strategies for building resilience include developing a growth mindset, setting realistic goals, and seeking support from others. Additionally, practicing self-care and maintaining a healthy work-life balance can enhance resilience by reducing stress and promoting overall well-being.

Effective communication is also crucial in overcoming resistance and building resilience. Clear, transparent, and empathetic communication can help address concerns, build trust, and create a sense of collaboration. By involving individuals in the decision-making process and providing regular updates, leaders can create a sense of ownership and buy-in, reducing resistance and fostering resilience.

Finally, fostering a positive and supportive environment can enhance resilience. Providing encouragement, recognizing achievements, and offering opportunities for growth and development can create a motivating and resilient atmosphere. This involves understanding the needs and preferences of individuals and creating an environment that supports their well-being and growth. By cultivating a positive and resilient environment, leaders can inspire others to overcome resistance and achieve their best.

10

Chapter 10: The Role of Empathy in Influence

Empathy is the ability to understand and share the feelings of others. It is a key component of effective influence and leadership, as it allows individuals to connect with others on a deeper level and build trust and rapport. In this chapter, we will explore the role of empathy in influence, highlighting its importance and providing practical tips for developing and practicing empathy.

Empathy involves both cognitive and emotional components. Cognitive empathy involves understanding the perspectives and emotions of others, while emotional empathy involves feeling and sharing those emotions. Both components are important for effective influence, as they allow individuals to connect with others and respond appropriately to their needs and concerns. Developing empathy involves actively listening, being open-minded, and practicing compassion and understanding.

Active listening is a crucial aspect of empathy. This involves giving your full attention to the speaker, asking clarifying questions, and providing feedback. Active listening demonstrates respect and understanding, and helps build trust and rapport. By truly listening to others, you can better understand their perspectives and emotions, and respond more effectively to their needs and concerns.

Being open-minded and non-judgmental is also important for practicing empathy. This involves recognizing and challenging your own biases and assumptions, and being willing to see things from different perspectives. By being open-minded and non-judgmental, you can create a more inclusive and empathetic environment, where individuals feel valued and understood.

Practicing compassion and understanding is another key aspect of empathy. This involves being kind, supportive, and considerate towards others, and recognizing their struggles and challenges. By showing compassion and understanding, you can build stronger connections and create a more supportive and empathetic environment. This not only enhances your ability to influence but also fosters a sense of community and collaboration.

11

Chapter 11: The Ethics of Influence

Influence is a powerful tool that comes with great responsibility. Ethical considerations are essential for ensuring that influence is used for positive and constructive purposes. In this chapter, we will explore the ethics of influence, highlighting key principles and providing practical tips for maintaining ethical standards in your influence and leadership practices.

Transparency is a fundamental principle of ethical influence. This involves being honest and open about your intentions, motivations, and goals. By being transparent, you build trust and credibility, and ensure that your influence is based on genuine and authentic interactions. Transparency also involves being clear and upfront about any potential conflicts of interest or biases, and ensuring that your actions are aligned with your values and principles.

Respect for autonomy is another key principle of ethical influence. This involves recognizing and honoring the autonomy and agency of others, and avoiding coercive or manipulative tactics. Ethical influence respects the rights and dignity of individuals, and seeks to empower rather than control. This involves providing information and options, and allowing individuals to make informed and voluntary decisions.

Accountability is also important for maintaining ethical standards in influence. This involves taking responsibility for your actions and their impact, and being willing to acknowledge and address any mistakes or shortcomings. This involves being transparent about your actions, seeking feedback, and being willing to make amends if necessary. Accountability fosters trust and ensures that influence is used responsibly and ethically.

Fairness and equity are also important principles of ethical influence. This involves treating others with respect and dignity, and ensuring that your actions do not disproportionately harm or disadvantage any individual or group. Ethical influence seeks to promote the well-being and interests of all parties involved, and avoids favoritism or discrimination. By promoting fairness and equity, you can build trust and create a positive and inclusive environment.

Finally, ethical influence involves a commitment to continuous learning and improvement. This involves staying informed about ethical standards and best practices, seeking feedback, and reflecting on your own actions and decisions. By continually striving to improve your ethical standards and practices, you can ensure that your influence remains positive and constructive.

12

Chapter 12: The Impact of Social Proof

Social proof is a powerful psychological phenomenon that influences behavior by leveraging the actions and opinions of others. It is based on the principle that people tend to follow the behavior of those they perceive as similar or credible. In this chapter, we will explore the impact of social proof on influence, highlighting key concepts and providing practical tips for leveraging social proof in your influence strategies.

Social proof can take various forms, such as testimonials, endorsements, and social media influence. Testimonials from satisfied customers or respected individuals can enhance credibility and trust, making others more likely to follow suit. Endorsements from experts or influencers can also have a significant impact, as they lend credibility and authority to the message. Social media influence, where individuals share their experiences and opinions online, can create a ripple effect, influencing the behavior of a larger audience.

Understanding the psychological mechanisms behind social proof is essential for leveraging it effectively. One key mechanism is the principle of similarity, where people are more likely to follow the behavior of those they perceive as similar to themselves. This involves highlighting commonalities and creating a sense of identification with the audience. Another mechanism is the principle of authority, where people are more likely to follow the behavior of those they perceive as credible or knowledgeable. This involves leveraging endorsements from respected individuals or organizations.

The use of social proof can be particularly effective in situations of uncertainty or ambiguity. When people are unsure about how to act or what decision to make, they often look to the behavior of others for guidance. By providing clear and credible examples of others' behavior, you can influence their decisions and actions. This can be achieved through various channels, such as customer reviews, case studies, and social media posts.

Ethical considerations are also important when using social proof. This involves ensuring that testimonials and endorsements are genuine and not misleading, and that social proof is used to promote positive and constructive behavior. By maintaining ethical standards, you can ensure that social proof is used responsibly and effectively.

13

Chapter 13: The Art of Negotiation

Negotiation is a critical skill for effective influence and leadership. It involves reaching agreements and resolving conflicts through communication and compromise. Successful negotiation requires understanding the needs and interests of all parties involved and finding mutually beneficial solutions. In this chapter, we will explore the art of negotiation, highlighting key strategies and providing practical tips for successful negotiation.

Preparation is the foundation of successful negotiation. This involves understanding your own goals and priorities, as well as those of the other parties involved. By being well-prepared, you can enter the negotiation with a clear understanding of what you want to achieve and what you are willing to compromise on. This also involves researching and gathering information about the other parties, such as their interests, needs, and potential constraints.

Effective communication is crucial in negotiation. This involves clearly articulating your own goals and interests, as well as actively listening to the other parties. By demonstrating empathy and understanding, you can build rapport and trust, which can facilitate a more collaborative and constructive negotiation process. Additionally, being open-minded and flexible can help you find creative solutions that meet the needs of all parties involved.

Finding common ground is another important aspect of negotiation. This involves identifying shared interests and goals, and using them as a basis for finding mutually beneficial solutions. By focusing on commonalities rather than differences, you can create a more positive and collaborative negotiation environment. This also involves being willing to compromise and finding win-win solutions that satisfy the needs of all parties involved.

Finally, maintaining a positive and respectful attitude is essential for successful negotiation. This involves being polite and professional, even in the face of disagreements or conflicts. By demonstrating respect and courtesy, you can create a more positive and productive negotiation environment. Additionally, being patient and persistent can help you navigate challenges and achieve a successful outcome.

14

Chapter 14: The Role of Emotional Intelligence in Influence

Emotional intelligence (EI) is the ability to understand and manage your own emotions, as well as the emotions of others. It is a key component of effective influence and leadership, as it allows individuals to connect with others on a deeper level and navigate complex social dynamics. In this chapter, we will explore the role of emotional intelligence in influence, highlighting its importance and providing practical tips for developing and practicing emotional intelligence.

Self-awareness is the foundation of emotional intelligence. This involves understanding your own emotions, strengths, and weaknesses, as well as how they impact your behavior and interactions with others. By being self-aware, you can better manage your emotions and respond more effectively to different situations. This involves reflecting on your experiences, seeking feedback from others, and being honest with yourself about your emotions and behaviors.

Self-regulation is another important aspect of emotional intelligence. This involves managing your own emotions and impulses, and staying calm and composed in challenging situations. By practicing self-regulation, you can avoid overreacting or making impulsive decisions, and maintain a positive and constructive attitude. This involves developing coping strategies, such as deep breathing, mindfulness, and positive self-talk, to manage stress and emotions effectively.

Social awareness, or the ability to understand the emotions and perspectives of others, is also crucial for emotional intelligence. This involves being empathetic and observant, and being able to read social cues and body language. By being socially aware, you can better understand the needs and concerns of others, and respond more effectively to their emotions. This involves actively listening, showing empathy, and being open-minded and non-judgmental.

Relationship management is the final component of emotional intelligence. This involves building and maintaining positive and constructive relationships with others, and effectively managing conflicts and disagreements. By practicing relationship management, you can build trust and rapport, and create a positive and collaborative environment. This involves being respectful and supportive, providing constructive feedback, and resolving conflicts in a fair and respectful manner.

15

Chapter 15: The Influence of Culture on Leadership

Culture plays a significant role in shaping leadership styles and practices. Different cultures have different values, norms, and expectations, which can impact how leadership is perceived and practiced. Understanding the influence of culture on leadership is essential for effective influence and leadership in a global and diverse world. In this chapter, we will explore the influence of culture on leadership, highlighting key concepts and providing practical tips for navigating cultural differences.

Cultural awareness is the foundation of understanding the influence of culture on leadership. This involves recognizing and appreciating the diversity of cultures and their impact on leadership styles and practices. By being culturally aware, you can better understand and respect the values and norms of different cultures, and adapt your leadership style accordingly. This involves being open-minded, curious, and respectful towards different cultures, and seeking to learn from and about them.

Adaptability is another important aspect of navigating cultural differences in leadership. This involves being flexible and willing to adjust your leadership style and practices to align with the cultural context. By being adaptable, you can build stronger relationships and enhance your influence in diverse settings. This involves being aware of cultural differences, seeking feedback from others, and being willing to learn and grow.

Effective communication is crucial for navigating cultural differences in leadership. This involves being clear and respectful in your communication, and being aware of potential cultural differences in communication styles. By being an effective communicator, you can avoid misunderstandings and build trust and rapport across cultures. This involves being an active listener, asking clarifying questions, and being open to feedback.

Respect for cultural diversity is also essential for effective leadership in a global and diverse world. This involves recognizing and valuing the unique contributions and perspectives of different cultures, and promoting an inclusive and respectful environment. By respecting cultural diversity, you can build stronger relationships and create a more positive and collaborative environment. This involves being inclusive, equitable, and respectful towards all individuals, regardless of their cultural background.

16

Chapter 16: The Role of Technology in Influence

Technology has transformed the way we communicate, connect, and influence others. From social media to digital marketing, technology provides powerful tools for reaching and engaging a wide audience. Understanding the role of technology in influence is essential for effective leadership in the digital age. In this chapter, we will explore the role of technology in influence, highlighting key concepts and providing practical tips for leveraging technology in your influence strategies.

Social media is a powerful tool for influence in the digital age. It allows individuals to connect with a large and diverse audience, share their message, and build their brand. By leveraging social media effectively, you can enhance your influence and reach a wider audience. This involves creating engaging content, building a strong online presence, and interacting with your audience. By being active and authentic on social media, you can build trust and credibility, and create a positive and influential online presence.

Digital marketing is another important aspect of influence in the digital age. This involves using various digital channels, such as email, social media, and search engines, to reach and engage your audience. By leveraging digital marketing strategies, you can enhance your influence and achieve your goals. This involves understanding your audience, creating targeted and relevant content, and using data and analytics to measure and optimize your strategies. By being strategic and data-driven in your digital marketing efforts, you can enhance your influence and achieve your desired outcomes.

Online collaboration tools are also crucial for effective leadership in the digital age. These tools allow individuals are transforming the way teams work together, even when they are physically distant. Tools like video conferencing, project management software, and collaborative document platforms enable real-time communication and collaboration, making it easier to coordinate efforts and achieve common goals. By leveraging online collaboration tools, leaders can enhance their influence and effectiveness, even in remote or distributed teams. This involves selecting the right tools for your team's needs, providing training and support, and fostering a culture of collaboration and communication.

The use of technology in influence also raises ethical considerations. This involves ensuring that technology is used responsibly and ethically, and that digital interactions are respectful and constructive. By maintaining ethical standards in your use of technology, you can build trust and credibility, and ensure that your influence is positive and constructive.

17

Chapter 17: Taking Action and Making a Difference

Influence is not just about persuading others but also about taking action and making a difference. Effective leaders and influencers are those who translate their vision and ideas into tangible results. In this final chapter, we will explore the importance of taking action and provide practical tips for turning your influence into meaningful impact.

Setting clear and achievable goals is the first step in taking action. This involves identifying what you want to achieve, breaking it down into manageable steps, and creating a plan for reaching your goals. By setting clear and specific goals, you can create a sense of direction and purpose, and stay focused on your objectives. Additionally, setting deadlines and creating accountability can enhance motivation and ensure that your goals are pursued with commitment and focus.

Taking initiative and being proactive is another important aspect of taking action. This involves being willing to step up and take responsibility, even in the face of challenges or uncertainty. By being proactive, you can create opportunities and drive progress, rather than waiting for things to happen. This involves being willing to take risks, make decisions, and act with confidence and determination.

Collaboration and teamwork are also crucial for turning influence into action. This involves working together with others, leveraging their strengths and expertise, and creating a sense of shared purpose and commitment. By fostering a collaborative and inclusive environment, you can enhance your influence and achieve your goals more effectively. This involves being respectful and supportive, providing constructive feedback, and recognizing and valuing the contributions of others.

Finally, reflecting on your actions and learning from your experiences is essential for continuous improvement. This involves seeking feedback, analyzing your successes and failures, and being willing to make adjustments and improvements. By continually reflecting and learning, you can enhance your influence and effectiveness, and make a positive and lasting impact.

In conclusion, the psychology of influence encompasses a wide range of principles and practices, from public speaking and leadership to communication and technology. By understanding and mastering these principles, individuals can enhance their ability to influence others, achieve their goals, and make a meaningful difference in their personal and professional lives.

"The Psychology of Influence: Public Speaking, Leadership, and the Art of Taking Action":

This book delves into the multifaceted world of influence, blending psychology, communication, and leadership principles to provide readers with a comprehensive guide to mastering the art of influence. From understanding the foundations of influence and the power of storytelling to exploring the dynamics of leadership and the role of empathy, this book offers practical insights and strategies for anyone looking to enhance their ability to influence others.

Each chapter provides a deep dive into a specific aspect of influence, such as the science of motivation, the art of persuasion, and the ethics of influence. The book also covers essential topics like public speaking, negotiation, and the impact of technology on influence, offering readers practical tips and techniques to apply in their personal and professional lives.

By combining theoretical knowledge with real-world examples and actionable advice, "The Psychology of Influence" empowers readers to take control of their influence, build strong relationships, and make a positive and lasting impact. Whether you're a leader, a public speaker, or simply someone looking to improve your communication skills, this book is an invaluable resource for understanding and mastering the psychology of influence.

www.ingramcontent.com/pod-product-compliance
Lightning Source LLC
LaVergne TN
LVHW020459080526
838202LV00057B/6047